SIMPLE
MAP READING

ROGER SMITH

SIMPLE
MAP READING

ROGER SMITH

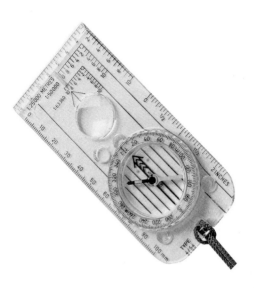

EDINBURGH: THE STATIONERY OFFICE

© The Stationery Office Limited 1997
First published 1997 by
The Stationery Office Limited, South Gyle Crescent,
Edinburgh EH12 9EB

Applications for reproduction should be made to
The Stationery Office Limited.

British Library Cataloguing in Publication Data

A catalogue record for this book is available from the
British Library

The author and publishers will welcome information on changes or
other helpful comments.

ISBN 0 11 495806 8

CONTENTS

ACKNOWLEDGEMENTS

The author and publishers would like to thank the following for their help in supplying illustrations for the book: Harvey Map Services Ltd (pp. 13, 18, 25, 32, 33, 47), London Underground (p.2), Ordnance Survey (pp. vii, 5, 7, 10, 11, 14, 16, 17, 19, 20, 21, 22, 24, 27, 28, 30, 41, 42, 46), Silva (UK) Ltd. (p. 31) and the United States Department of the Interior Geological Survey (p. 51). Cover map courtesy Harvey Map Services Ltd. Cover compass courtesy Silva (UK) Ltd. Although facts have been checked as carefully as possible, the author and publishers can accept no responsibility for errors, however caused.

Extract from an old Ordnance Survey map.

© Crown Copyright

1 WHAT IS A MAP?

Ever since we began journeying and exploring this planet many thousands of years ago, we have felt the need to map our journeys, both as a record of where we have been and what we saw there, and also as a guide for others. Among the earliest attempts at mapping were those by Greek, Roman and Phoenician navigators who covered great distances looking for new lands to conquer or trade with.

Venturing out of the relative safety of the Mediterranean, they turned both north and south, voyaging to Britain (and perhaps beyond) and also down the coast of Africa. Navigating by the stars, which were recognised as having a constant pattern, they returned with tales of strange and exotic lands and put representations of those lands, and the seas around them, on to papyrus or paper so that others might follow.

What they were aiming to do then is no different from the aim of the cartographer today: the art of capturing on a flat, two-dimensional sheet of paper, a true representation of part of a three-dimensional world that is, moreover, a flattened sphere. The mapmaker has to place himself metaphorically above the area being mapped and try to imagine what it looks like.

On a very small scale, this is not too difficult. You can do it by making a map of the room you are in, measuring the walls and where the furniture is and showing them on your map. It is as if you are looking down from the ceiling on what is below. The art, however, is getting everything both in scale and in proportion, and the further you spread out from the single room, the more difficult this becomes.

Mapmakers have developed ways of overcoming the difficulties, so that we now have accurate maps of everything from sewer systems in our cities to national boundaries and whole continents. Mapmakers flatten the earth and spread it out, so that we understand the spatial relationship between countries, continents and oceans. On a more local scale, they show us how we can get from any place in our own country to any other place, and from street to street within towns. Those who enjoy the hills are able to navigate safely using the large-scale maps produced by the Ordnance Survey, by Harveys, and by other mapmakers. Maps are an important part of our lives.

From the earliest times, maps were prepared for different purposes. The early seafarers needed to know the characteristics of the coasts around which they sailed, so their maps concentrate on dangerous headlands, rocks and currents. Traders needed the location of settlements where they could buy or sell goods, and the tracks between them: the surrounding countryside was less important, and on early maps there are often large gaps, sometimes filled with wonderfully fanciful legends such as "here be dragons".

The same principles apply today. A road map does not show you the nature of the countryside, apart from a fairly crude representation of steep gradients on the roads themselves and an indication of major features such as lakes. Street maps of towns, though invaluable, are often even more basic, and may not even be to scale. What is important is the name of the street you are looking for, and its general location.

A good example of a brilliantly specialised map which is used by millions of people each year, its design taken for granted, is the stylised route map of the London Underground. The

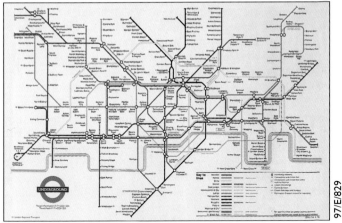

97/E/829

Map of the London Underground.

designer, Henry Beck, realised that scale and accurate orientation were not important: travellers needed a clear indication of the different lines, where they intersected, and the station names. Even the River Thames became a caricature of its true self. His 1933 design, with a different colour-code for each line, was so successful that it survives today and has been copied for many other cities across the world.

Despite the highly stylised nature of his map, Beck still held true to the best cartographic principles. He concentrated on what was important to the map user and made sure that information was presented with clarity. You can find what you want on his map at a glance. The same should be true of all maps, and a basic requirement for this is that the map user should readily understand the symbols used to depict the various features shown on the map.

Many of these are standardised and quite familiar to us. Water is shown in blue, forests in green, contour relief (height and gradient) in brown, rock features in black, built-up areas in orange and so on. There are, however, many other symbols which are used on maps and which can help you both to understand the map and to get more useful information from it. These symbols are looked at in more detail in Chapter 3.

Another basic of most maps is the scale to which they are drawn. The Underground map only needs to be to scale in the sense of showing that, say, King's Cross is further from Earl's Court than it is from Piccadilly. Most maps are drawn to a consistent scale, and understanding what that scale is assists the user. Scale is looked at in Chapter 2.

The book goes on to look at other map features such as the National Grid, characteristics of road maps and how to use them, the compass, maps in other countries, introducing maps to children, and generally tries to encourage the reader to become familiar with maps and enjoy using them.

I freely confess to being a map freak. I read maps in the evening or at weekends the way other people read books, and I get just as much enjoyment from them. The story they tell, once you know how to unravel it, is endlessly fascinating, and they provide both clues to the history and nature of the area they cover, and encouragement to go out and explore for yourself. There are always things to be discovered, and maps help you find them.

Most of us use maps regularly, while driving, travelling by train or bus, or perhaps walking in our local area. I suspect that most of us also don't get as much out of maps as we might, and this book aims to introduce the fascinating subject of maps and mapping and to show that maps are wonderful tools which we can all enjoy using and from which we can get great pleasure and benefit.

2 MAKING MAPS: THE ORDNANCE SURVEY

How are maps made? From the earliest times, the basic system has not changed. It is a matter of gathering information, collating and assessing it, and then transferring it as accurately as possible on to paper. The technology has changed quite remarkably, and most maps are now originated on computer, but the fundamental principles are the same.

We are used to having very accurate maps to help us get around, whether by car, public transport or on foot, but such maps are a relatively recent development, and surveying itself – gathering the vital information needed for the map – was also a fairly crude art not that long ago.

After his victory at the Battle of Culloden in 1746, the Duke of Cumberland, on behalf of his officers, complained to his father, King George II, that they had been "embarrassed for want of a proper survey of the country". The result was that General William Roy was commissioned to undertake a survey of Scotland and produce good maps of the whole country.

The survey took place between 1747 and 1755, and although the resulting maps, at the rather odd scale of 1:36 000, were described modestly by Roy as "rather a magnificent military sketch than a very accurate map", they were still a vast improvement on what hade been available previously.

Forty years later, at the other end of Britain, the government found themselves again in need of good maps for strategic reasons. This time it was the threat of a Napoleonic invasion from France which triggered the survey, and led in 1791 to the formation of the Ordnance Survey, in order to produce accurate maps of the south coast of England so that defences could be properly planned.

The name Ordnance Survey has appeared on our maps ever since, and we take it for granted, but a quick look at the name reveals its origins. The dictionary defines "ordnance" as "a department concerned with the supply and maintenance of artillery". In other words, it is part of the Army, and the original Ordnance Survey was, quite simply, a survey undertaken by the

Board of Ordnance – the body responsible for equipping the Army. The OS remained part of the Board of Ordnance until 1889, by which time it had long ceased to be primarily a military operation and had instead become, as it still is today, Britain's national mapping agency.

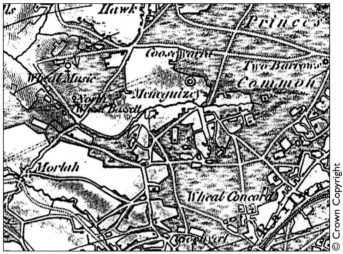

© Crown Copyright

Extract from an early Ordnance Survey map.

From the original survey of the south coast begun in the 1790s, the mapmakers went on to cover the whole country on a properly accurate and scientific basis. In order to do this, they needed fixed points which could be constantly referred to and relied on as being accurate. If, wherever you are, you can take a bearing on two such points, you can establish your position with reasonable accuracy.

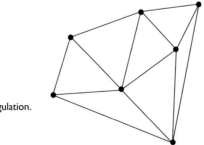

Triangulation.

You thus end up with a continuous system of triangles, and triangulation was indeed the basis of measurement used. Your fixed points naturally need to be intervisible (always seen one from the other) and thus are mostly on high places. This brilliantly simple idea proved to be effective, and led in time to the setting up of the stone triangulation pillars which are such a familiar feature of hilltops today.

Most of these pillars are in fact now redundant, as mapping methods have moved on to the use of global positioning satellites (GPS) which orbit the earth in fixed locations and continuously transmit data for use in modern mapping. We are thus back with the original concept introduced at the start of Chapter 1, that of a map being a view of the terrain from above.

We are lucky in the UK in that our maps, produced by the Ordnance Survey (and increasingly by other mapmakers), are of a consistently high quality. We also have a variety of scales available, designed to suit different needs.

The most familiar maps to most of us will be the Ordnance Survey's 1:50 000 Landranger series (red covers) and 1:25 000 Pathfinder series (green covers), Outdoor Leisure maps (yellow covers) and Explorer maps (orange covers). These two scales cover the whole country, and are regularly updated. It is a mark of how useful these maps are and how much they are used, that some 2 million Landranger maps are sold each year. As there are 204 sheets, this represents an average sale of 10,000 copies per map. The sale in fact varies from over 30,000 for the most popular maps to under 5000 for a few maps of remote areas. On average, 40 of these maps are revised and reissued each year. In spring 1996, OS announced a series of "enhancements" to Landranger maps, and provided more in the way of useful information, especially for walkers and cyclists.

The 1:50 000 series is a metric evolution of the former 1-inch to the miles (1:63 360) maps which were the first really popular OS maps to be produced. At one time they were printed on cloth, and these much-loved maps are still cherished by map collectors. When the change was made in the 1970s, the first 1:50 000 maps were simply photographically enlarged 1-inch maps, but full revision has now taken place, with the contour interval altered from the former 50 feet to 10 metres, enabling more detail to be shown in hilly areas.

Similarly, the 1:25 000 maps are an evolution of the former $2^1/_2$-inch to the mile series (the scale is only slightly different). These maps are much used by walkers for the greater detail they are able to show, including field boundaries. Sales have been encouraged by the introduction of enhanced maps of popular areas, first as the Outdoor Leisure series. There are now over 40 of these maps, covering national parks and other popular areas;

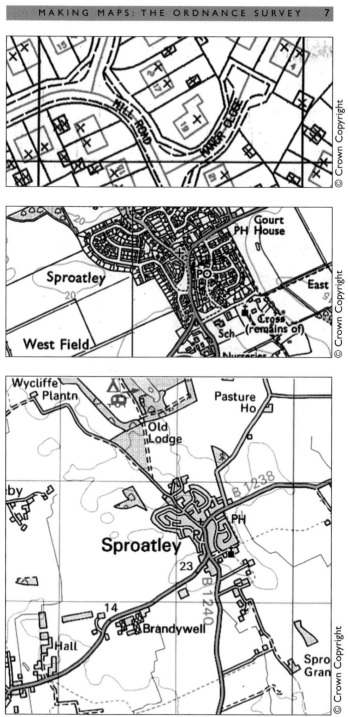

© Crown Copyright

© Crown Copyright

© Crown Copyright

Extracts from Ordnance Survey maps of different scales: (top to bottom)
1:2500 scale; 1:25 000 scale; and 1:50 000 scale.

some are printed double-sided for extra coverage (and economy in production). They include extra information for visitors, walkers and cyclists and sell consistently well.

A more recent innovation has been the Explorer maps. These are basically two Pathfinders printed together with some extra information added – again providing improved value for money. OS announced in autumn 1997 that in order to ensure that the whole of Britain continues to be covered at 1:25 000, the Pathfinder series, many of which sell only in very small numbers, will be replaced by Explorer maps by 2002. The 1:50 000 Landranger series will continue as at present.

OS also provide comprehensive coverage at 1:10 000 and even, in urban areas, at 1:2500. These large scales are useful to professionals such as surveyors, road and water engineers and the like. All of these maps are now computer-generated and can be customised on request. The Ordnance Survey, formerly a government department, is currently what is called a Next Steps Agency, and although still receiving a small amount of central support (about £15 million in 1997) has to generate most of its income itself through its map sales and other commercial activities. These have diversified remarkably, and you can now, for example, get CD-Rom coverage of the UK, principally sold for educational purposes.

In practical terms, most of us will happily go on using paper maps at the familiar 1:50 000 and 1:25 000 scales, and this book aims to help you to understand these maps and to show you how to be confident in their use. They are wonderful companions and reliable guides.

3 A LOOK AT SCALES

Most maps are drawn to scale – that is, the distance between points on the map is an accurate representation of the distance between the same points on the ground. You should always be aware of the scale of the map you are using; without this information, you are operating by guesswork.

As an example, in the diagrams below the two towns, Oldtown and Newtown, are 10 cm (4 in) apart on the map, with a straight road joining them. Without knowing what distance those 10 cm represent, you don't know how far it is between the two towns, and cannot therefore estimate your journey time. They could be 10 km apart, or 100 km.

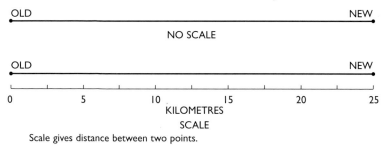

Scale gives distance between two points.

In the second diagram, a scale has been added, and you see that 1 cm on the map equals 2.5 km on the ground, a scale of 1:250 000 (not unusual in road maps). You can now easily work out that Oldtown and Newtown are 25 km apart, and plan your journey accordingly. On many road maps, of course, this information will be supplied, at least for the major roads, but it is always useful to be able to work it out easily for yourself, and knowing the scale enables you to do that.

Scale is also useful in geographical and topographical terms for showing not just the distance between features or points, but the size of particular features. Many people have had the experience of puzzling over a scaleless map supplied in a travel brochure, trying to work out the size of the area they were visiting. A simple scale would have helped greatly.

Scale is the only feature on maps which is three-dimensional. The symbol for a building gives no indication of how tall that building is, but the contour lines on a map do show how the land itself rises and falls. Contours are considered in more detail in Chapter 4; on British maps, height is always shown as above mean sea level at a fixed point on the coast (currently Newlyn in Cornwall), and you are also helped by frequent "spot" height checks for hilltops. Contours are very important when planning routes across country on foot, cycle or horseback.

Although you are less likely to use them, it is also worth noting that "contours" (technically called "isobaths") are also shown on large water features to indicate the depth of water. All this information is part of the element of scale on a map.

The previous chapter showed how the whole of the UK is covered by Ordnance Survey maps at different scales. Many popular walking areas also have Harvey maps available, at 1:40 000 and/or 1:25 000. A fundamental point to remember is that, regardless of the scale, the "grid squares" on the map have sides of 1 km. The square on a 1:25 000 scale map will therefore be four times as big as the square covering the same piece of ground on a 1:50 000

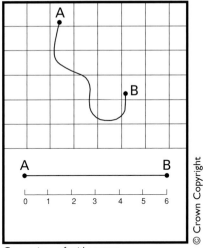

Comparison of grid squares.

© Crown Copyright

map. The grid squares on the larger scale maps – 1:10 000 or, in towns, even 1:2500 – are less important in terms of measuring distance but are still used by surveyors. A marginal scale on such maps helps with accurate measurement, which on the biggest and most detailed maps can be calculated to the nearest metre.

The grid squares on the commonly-used maps (1:50 000 and 1:25 000) can be used to calculate distance even when you are not travelling in a straight line. You can measure from point A to point B using a piece of string or cotton, or (if you have one) a map measurer, which uses a little wheel that you run over the map, following your route.

Assuming you are using the "string" method, run the string along your route as carefully as you can. Then all you have to do is lay the string along any grid line on the map and count off the 1 km squares, to get your distance. In time, with plenty of practice, you can do this by eye, and with the experienced traveller, this quickly translates into a good estimate of journey time.

Understanding scale is a very worthwhile skill to acquire, and it can only really be done by practice. Keep trying it every time you go out and you will be surprised at how quickly it becomes second nature. Many experienced hillwalkers can predict journey time (excluding unforeseen circumstances, of course) very accurately, enabling outings to be tied in to times of public transport or, more importantly in winter, the hours of daylight.

Scale on maps is also closely related to the detail that can be shown. The larger the scale, the more detail you can get in

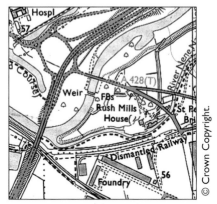

Extract from 1:25 000 map showing field boundaries.

without unduly cluttering the map. On a normal road map, it is almost impossible to show individual features such as buildings. Even on 1:50 000 maps, many areas of housing are shown simply as blocks of orange tone. Individual houses in rural areas are often shown, as are large public buildings such as churches and town halls.

At 1:25 000, it is easier to show houses separately, and at this scale, much more in the way of useful detail generally is included – one of the most important attributes of the 1:25 000

Map scale	Distance on map	Distance on ground
1:10 000	1 cm	100 m
	5 cm	500 m
	10 cm	1 km
	1 inch	277.77 yds
	6 ins	1666.66 yds
	6.33 ins	1 mile
1:25 000	1 cm	250 m
	4 cm	1 km
	10 cm	2.5 km
	1 inch	695 yds
	2.534 ins	1 mile
1:50 000	1 cm	500 m
	2 cm	1 km
	10 cm	5 km
	1 inch	1390 yds
	1.267 ins	1 mile
1:100 000	1 cm	1 km
	10 cm	10 km
	0.633 ins	1 mile

The relationship between scales and distances.

maps for the walker is that they show field boundaries. They do not differentiate between fences, hedges and walls, however, and you need to be aware that the countryside is dynamic, and that these boundaries tend to change over time, but their depiction on the map is still extremely useful, as are smaller features within woodland areas such as rides and firebreaks.

Although OS maps are generally very accurate, in order to make some features stand out properly, one or more of their dimensions may be exaggerated. This applies to roads, which are often shown wider on the map than they are on the ground, just so that they stand out. It also applies to symbols for some "point" features, which have to be drawn so that you can read them.

The blue symbol for a triangulation pillar shows where the pillar is, not its size (less than 1 m square). The actual position of the pillar should be shown by the centre of the symbol, so that you can still use it for measuring purposes, and this also applies to other point features.

The table above shows how scales relate to distances on the map itself, in both metric and Imperial terms. From now on, every time you look at a map, look first of all for its scale, and as an initial practice exercise, try to use the scale to estimate distance between a few points on the map. Keep doing this until your estimates are consistently reasonably accurate.

You will probably be using one of the common OS scales, most likely 1:50 000, to begin with, and it is certainly worth getting used to judging distance using one scale before moving on to

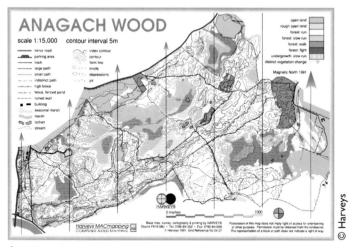

An orienteering map.

another. Most regular map users are fairly well used to judging distance using both 1:25 000 and 1:50 000. People who enjoy the navigational sport of orienteering have to get used to differing scales. The sport uses very detailed maps at 1:10 000 and 1:15 000, and perhaps 1:20 000 for larger areas. Today, one of the main competitors to the OS, Harvey Map Services, who produce excellent maps principally of mountain areas, use 1:40 000 as one of their basic scales because they feel it is better for showing contour detail and relief.

Another valuable exercise relating to scale is to take a map out with you and, having established your present position, try to estimate how far away things are that you can see. Make sure that they are features shown on the map, such as a bridge, wood or large individual building. Surprisingly quickly you begin to make accurate estimates. This in turn enables you the better to "place" yourself in the landscape. In hill country this skill is invaluable, particularly if the terrain is undulating and relatively featureless.

This chapter has tried to show you how important scale is, and why the scale should be among the first things you look for every time you pick up a map.

4 FINDING YOUR WAY

It is now time to begin to look at how to use a map. First of all, don't be afraid of it. The map is your friend, giving you lots of helpful information and helping you plan routes, find your way around and generally learn more about our fascinating history, landscape and countryside.

It largely does this by the use of *symbols* – internationally-understood signs and marks in particular colours which bring the map to life and are very much the pictorial language of mapping and mapmakers. The picture varies tremendously according to the nature of the area.

For instance, large-scale maps covering the Greater London area show dense patterns of housing and road networks, with relatively few contour lines indicating height. Even on these maps, there is a pleasing amount of open space, indicated either by white, or green for woodland.

By contrast, on maps of the same scale covering the West Highlands of Scotland, in an area of 400 square km there is just one road, with a railway paralleling it, a few tracks, perhaps a dozen inhabited buildings – but a mass of contour lines and rock symbols, a lot of water and several large patches of forestry.

All maps are interesting – once you know how to interpret them, there is no such thing as a boring area of landscape. Map study will always reveal things of interest worth exploring and discovering, and again, the symbols are the key to this. They are all shown in the "legend" at the right-hand side of OS sheets, and it is worth spending some time studying this legend until you are familiar with the main symbols.

You will see that they break down into a number of colour patterns. As the simplest examples, contours showing

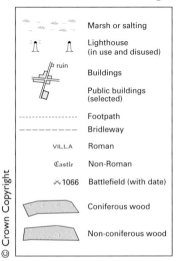

	Marsh or salting
	Lighthouse (in use and disused)
	Buildings
	Public buildings (selected)
	Footpath
	Bridleway
VILLA	Roman
Castle	Non-Roman
✕1066	Battlefield (with date)
	Coniferous wood
	Non-coniferous wood

Basic map symbols.

height and landform are brown, water features are blue and woodland is green. Open land, whether cultivated or not, is left white (there is an interesting argument as to whether larger scale maps should show cultivated fields in yellow, but given the changing nature of the countryside, this might be difficult to keep up to date).

All these symbols are relatively easy to spot. There are some exceptions or "rogues" in there, however. Triangulation pillars, mostly found on hilltops, are shown in blue, as are the "tourist information" symbols such as picnic sites, viewpoints and car parks. All these are definitely non-watery, as are motorways.

The two main blocks of symbols not mentioned yet are those for lines of communications – roads, tracks, paths, railways and also power lines. The latter two, railways and power lines, are shown in black, the power lines being a finer line with small "v" symbols along their length. Note that only main grid lines on pylons are shown, not local lines. One area which may cause initial confusion is that pipelines, generally underground and thus not visible, are shown as dashed black lines with arrows.

Roads are depicted in a variety of colours. Motorways are shown in blue, with black boundaries, and are also identified by their number, as are all classified roads. A-class roads are red and B-class are orange. In both cases, if the road is single-track with passing places, white spaces are added along the road. Minor roads below B-class, but still public highways, are shown in yellow. It is worth noting that width is representational on roads. To make them stand out better, they are shown wider than they actually are in many cases.

Tracks which could still be used by vehicles (though often only by tractors, 4WD or the like) are shown in white, with either solid or dotted edges to indicated fenced or unfenced. Footpaths are shown as a single dashed black line (public rights of way have various symbols – see access, Chapter 11).

In addition to the symbols described above, Harvey maps aim to show farmland and different types of vegetation cover. Open fields are solid yellow, rough pasture is a light yellow, and according to how open it is, woodland is denoted by different densities of green. These shadings are very helpful in route-planning: it is obviously easier to walk through open woodland than to struggle through a dense conifer plantation.

These yellow and green shadings originated in the specialised world of orienteering maps. The sport of orienteering demands that competitors cover the ground as rapidly as possible while navigating, and it is vital that they know exactly what is ahead of them. Woodland is graded from "clear" to "fight", the last category leaving nothing to the imagination!

Harveys have been leaders in orienteering maps for 25 years, and have put this long experience to good use in producing maps for more general use.

This brief run-through covers the main symbols that you need to recognise and use. It is probably best to start finding your way around using a map by using only the easiest of symbols – those for roads and perhaps tracks. Many a good outing can be planned, on foot or cycle, using minor roads and lanes before moving on to footpaths or open country.

You can plan circular routes from your home, expeditions back to home from a distant point, or circular expeditions from somewhere you are keen to visit. Keep the length of outing and time taken manageable to start with, a couple of hours or so, and try to plan routes which take you past or near a good variety of features shown by different map symbols.

Although you are safely on roads or tracks, you can pass or see water features of different kinds, power lines, woods, buildings, bridges and so on. All of this will help you become familiar with the map and its symbols.

Features shown on maps are of two main types – *line* or *point*. These terms largely explain themselves. *Line* features are those which extend for a distance across the map. This category therefore includes all roads, tracks and paths, long bridges, railways, watercourses, contours, and power lines.

However, places where such features intersect can be classed as *point* features – a road junction is a definite point and can be clearly identified as such by means of its grid reference (Chapter 7). Other point features on maps include individual

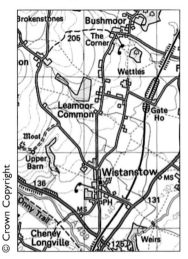

© Crown Copyright

Example of linear features.

buildings, short bridges, railway and bus stations, triangulation pillars, radio masts and so on.

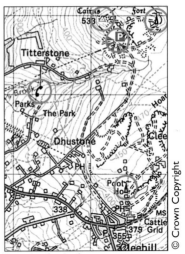

There are things shown on maps which are *areal* (covering large areas) and fall into neither the point nor line category. The most obvious of these are woods and forests. However, their edges and boundaries, often clearly marked, are line features. Other areal features include substantial areas of housing and large sheets of water such as lakes.

Example of point features.

Your route planning will involve the use of both main types of features. The way you travel will generally be along line features such as roads and tracks, but you will note significant point features along the way to act as landmarks and guides.

Now that you are starting to look at the map more closely and plan outings using it, it is worth acquiring the important skill of *setting the map*. This merely means adjusting the way you hold map so that what you see ahead of you is also "ahead" on the map, and it can help greatly to keep you right on your outings.

All our maps are aligned to grid north, which is always at the top of the map. But, of course, when you are out using the map, you are only rarely travelling north. If you hold the map in front of you with north at the top, you are thus unlikely to have the map aligned to your direction of travel.

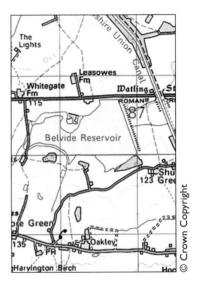

This alignment is achieved in one of two ways. It can be done using a compass, and that method is covered in

Example of areal features.

Chapter 8. It can also be done by relating what you see on the ground to what you see on the map. If you are on a road, and are quite certain of your position, you can move the map around, until the road on the map points directly away from you, following the course of the road on the ground. You can do the same with any other line feature. Once you are sure you have it right, the map is aligned or "set" and the features on the ground should follow the same pattern as shown on the map. This helps you identify easily what lies ahead, and the significant points you are approaching.

Do take care that north on the map aligns with north on the ground. You should know in which direction you are travelling even without a compass, by points you have passed or are approaching, and can thus align the map accordingly.

After an explanation of contours and the way they show height and landform, planning expeditions with a map is covered in more detail, to begin to help you get the most from your outings and from the maps you use.

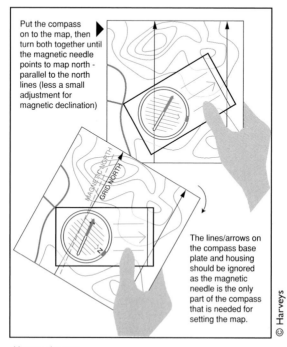

Put the compass on to the map, then turn both together until the magnetic needle points to map north - parallel to the north lines (less a small adjustment for magnetic declination)

The lines/arrows on the compass base plate and housing should be ignored as the magnetic needle is the only part of the compass that is needed for setting the map.

© Harveys

Aligning the map.

5 READING CONTOURS

The main map symbols representing such familiar things as roads, tracks, rivers, buildings and woodland have now been explained, and you should have practised using them to the point where you can recognise them as soon as you see them on the map. There are, however, large areas of many maps which are principally covered not with these symbols, but with a mass of brown lines.

Curving, twisting, sometimes packed together, sometimes well spaced, they may at first sight look impossible to decipher. They are among the most important symbols on any map, and are the key to planning and enjoying many journeys.

These brown lines are called *contours*. The word comes from a European root meaning to surround or outline, and contours are just that – an outline of the shape of the land. Contours join places of equal height above sea level. On older 1-inch to the mile OS maps, the lines were drawn every 50 ft, so that contours were shown at 250 ft, 300 ft, 350 ft and so on. This is known as the "contour interval". On today's metric OS maps, the interval has been reduced to 10 m, allowing finer detail to be shown. Harvey maps have contours at 15 m intervals; always check the map legend to see what the contour interval is, as this will help you to "read" the steepness of the ground.

There are in fact many kinds of "contours" that can be shown on specialist maps, indicating places of equal rainfall, temperature, pressure and so on, but those showing height and landform are the only ones you are likely to use.

They are not difficult to understand, and are presented very logically. As an example, take a

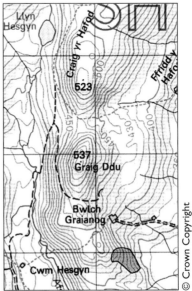

Examples of contour lines.

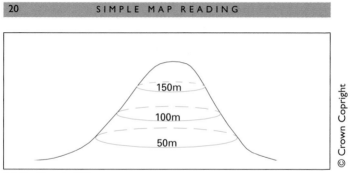

A "sliced" conical hill.

perfectly conical hill 205 m high, tapering evenly to its summit. If you slice through it at 10-m intervals, going up, you are slicing along the contour lines, and you will be left with a series of circles of steadily decreasing circumference until you cut off the last one, at 200 m, leaving you finally with a very small cone representing the summit of the hill.

This last point is worth underlining. The contour interval is 10 m (33 ft), which means that features within the 10-m range may not be shown. A fairly substantial bump 8 m (25 ft) high on the side of the hill could thus quite legitimately be omitted from the map, so don't expect contours to show every little indentation or excrescence.

If all hills were perfectly conical, the contours would be very easy to read. Life's much more fun than that, however, and hills come in all shapes and sizes. A very important factor in reading

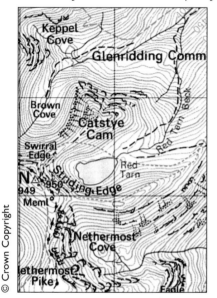

contours is to look at the water features, shown in blue. Streams and rivers run down valleys, from high ground to low, and the contours curve around them, as shown here. It follows that the contours are rising either side of the stream until they reach a high point or ridge between the streams. This kind of stream-ridge-stream pattern is very common in the British country-side, and one of the

A ridge and valley pattern.

commonest map reading errors is to misread it, so that you think you should be going up when you are in fact going down.

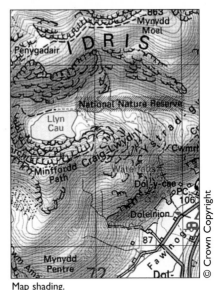

To assist you further, significant contours are both strengthened in thickness and numbered. This generally happens every 50 m. And, of course, almost all our hills are named, the showing of the name at the hill top again helping recognition of the contour pattern (and increasing interest – all

Map shading.

these names are significant in one way or another). Triangulation pillars are also on higher ground, as a further aid.

The *spacing* of contours is another important thing to look for. The principle is simple – the closer together the contours, the steeper the slope, and thus the tougher the climb. When the slope becomes too steep for the contours to be shown individually, cliff or rock symbols may be used instead. These are places to be avoided, so contour recognition is important in safety terms.

Some maps have attempted to show this more pictorially by the use of *shading*, varying the colours according to the height and/or steepness. European maps in areas such as the Alps use shading to dramatic effect, and it has also been used in the UK by mapmakers including Bartholomews. The OS experimented with hill shading on a Landranger map of the Dolgellau area of North Wales in 1994, but after considering reaction from map users, decided not to proceed with it on a wider basis.

There are two common patterns of hill slopes, which you should learn to recognise – *convex* and *concave*, as shown in the diagram on p.22. In *convex* slopes, the hill bulges outwards. The steeper slopes are at the lower level, with the slope lessening as the summit is neared. This means that as you start the climb you can't see the top of the hill, which only becomes visible higher up as the slope falls back.

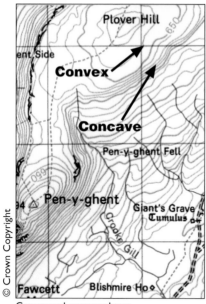

Convex and concave slopes.

In *concave* slopes, the picture is reversed. You can often see the summit from much lower down, but as you draw nearer to it, the slope steepens and it may become hidden from view until almost the last moment. Concave hills are often more dangerous, especially in winter when unstable masses of snow can accumulate on the steeper, higher sections.

You will notice that some of the contours are circular. These are known as "ring contours" and are generally found on hill tops or plateau areas. They still join points of equal height but either there is no higher point, or they represent a small bump on an otherwise flat area. Ring contours can also be found, though more rarely, in broad, flat-bottomed valleys.

Recognising landforms through reading contours is a very worthwhile skill to acquire, and is pretty well essential if you are planning cross-country journeys on foot (or by bike) of any distance. You learn to plan your journey avoiding the steepest slopes and minimising the ascent. This is covered further in Chapter 9.

In the navigational sport of orienteering, a common training exercise is to give orienteers a map which only shows contours – no roads, tracks or buildings, and no water features – and ask them to navigate using solely the brown lines. It teaches you very quickly to sort out uphill from down, and to recognise contour "patterns" showing the landform.

In the same way, integrating contours into your map-reading will help you get a full mental picture of the landscape and a greater understanding of the area you are traversing.

6 GOING OUT WITH A MAP

Now that some of the basics of maps have been covered, it's time to put the theory into practice. There is no substitute for actually going out and using a map, but a little planning is helpful before any expedition (this also applies to car journeys – see Chapter 10).

I would make two suggestions at this stage, for those unused to going out with a map. Firstly, start with your home area; and secondly, if you can, get copies of both the Ordnance Survey 1:50 000 Landranger and 1:25 000 Pathfinder (or Outdoor Leisure or Explorer) series maps for your area, or the Harvey map if there is one.

It should help starting with your home area for several reasons. You will already be familiar with many of the places and features shown on the map, and will be able to "place" yourself on the map more easily as a result. You can start by making small expeditions from your home – and of course this will be less expensive than travelling further away.

A third suggestion would be to make a plan and stick to it. For the less experienced map user, changing plans in mid-route is only likely to lead to confusion. Flexibility is a very worthwhile attribute, but it can come into the frame later on when you are more confident with the map.

For your first outings, either plan a short route from your home or – and this might be more interesting, particularly if children are involved – take public transport to somewhere not too far away and work your way back from it. Using the transport for the outward leg is definitely preferred as you are then making your way back towards the goal of your home (the same applies if you are fortunate enough to have a willing driver who can take you out). The alternative, walking out to a destination point, is not as good as unless you have timed things particularly well, you may have to wait around for return transport, which rather takes the edge off the expedition.

If this truly is your first outing with a map, choose a very simple route, preferably with a number of unmissable features along the way. These might include road junctions, bridges, landmark buildings or specific and easily recognised areas such as parks. If you can walk back along a river or canal using a footpath, that's fine. Try to avoid main roads as they don't all have pavements or footpaths along them (unless you are staying within a town boundary). If you live near a railway line, consider going to the next station and making your way back from there (but not if it's 30 miles away!).

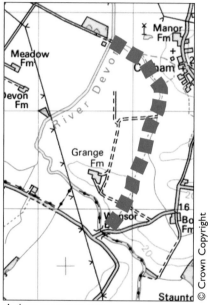

A short route on a map.

Looking at the map and working out an easy route to follow is all part of the exercise, and remember that every time you do this, you are becoming more familiar with the map and its features. Another option for early outings is to use a well-marked footpath or trail. You can find these in many parts of the country; the major ones are marked on OS maps, but it can be just as much fun following, say, a circular forest trail which is colour-coded so that you can't really get lost, but instead of relying totally on the waymarking, try to follow the trail on your map.

I advised earlier getting both the Landranger/Explorer and Pathfinder maps. This enables you to start getting familiar with using both scales, helps you relate one to the other, and on your early outings which are likely to be fairly short in terms of distance, the extra detail on the Pathfinder will be a great help and give you more confidence.

ROUTE CARD

Feature	Route	Distance	Time
Car park			
	Footpath through forest		
	Uphill	1100m	
A Forest edge			
	Footpath to ridge		
	Uphill	950m	
B Ridge			
	Footpath to summit		
	Uphill	1500m	
C Summit			
	Ridge to saddle		
	No path, old fence		
	Downhill	1250m	
D Saddle			
	Footpath to large boulders		
	Downhill	1100m	
E Boulders			
	Footpath (crossing two roads)		
	Waterfall to visit on the left		
	Downhill	1500m	
F Bridge			
	Road back to car park		
	Level	1400m	
G Car park			
	TOTAL DISTANCE	8800m	

© Harveys

One point to bear in mind is that, unless you live in an area where they sell well, or are using a yellow OL map, Pathfinders/Explorers tend to be revised less often than Landrangers. You may therefore find (as I do with my own home area) that quite important features such as new roads and recent housing developments are not shown. Always check the revision date in the map margin. This does not stop you using the map, but it is a point to bear in mind.

Even in poor weather conditions, you can continue your map practice by taking it with you in the car. It can be great fun, especially for children, to go to a place you've never visited before and then make your way back, taking your time and using the map as much as possible. It should, of course, only be the passengers who use the map, not the driver! Stop as often

as you like to check your position and "orientate" yourself to places and features around you.

Every time you go out, you will be adding to your experience in terms of confidence in handling the map, familiarity with map symbols, recognition of scale, estimation of journey time, and good route planning. Keep your maps handy and take them out as often as you can.

Once you have become reasonably familiar with your home area you can, if you like, start planning outings to places further away. Always follow the same "plan of campaign". Find a route you would like to follow, perhaps centred on something interesting like a castle, waterfall or hilltop. Plan the route carefully at home (mark it on the map in pencil if you want, or write down the main features of it as a "'route plan"), and try to estimate (a) how long it will take you, and (b) what are the main points you expect to see along the way – your landmark features.

Then go out and enjoy following the route you have planned. If you are walking, a reasonable average speed without hurrying is 2 miles, or 3 km, per hour.

7 THE NATIONAL GRID

It is an interesting thought that, if things had gone differently, we might all be using national grid references on a daily basis, instead of only rarely. In the 1940s there was a serious proposal that all properties in the UK should be identified by their national grid reference as part of their full address – a kind of postcode, in fact.

It's quite a logical idea – after all, the grid references were already all in place, whereas the postcode system we now use has had to be devised. An additional advantage would have been that your address could be found on a map, even if the map did not name streets. Postcodes do not appear on any map, but grid references do. However, it was not to be, and grid references remain something of a mystery to many people. This is a pity as they are in fact very useful, and not at all difficult to work out and use.

The basic concept is a simple one: the whole of the UK is divided, on large-scale maps, into numbered "grid squares" with sides measuring 1 km. The grid numbers are called "eastings" – those that go across the map from west to east – and "northings"– those that run up the map from south to north.

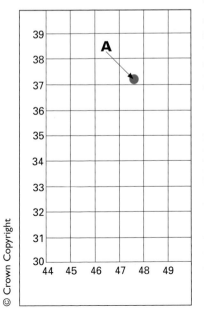

These numbers, which are all two-figured (between 00 and 99) are shown around the margin of the map and also overprinted on it at regular intervals, in light blue.

It can be seen that the numerical references will repeat themselves every 100 km. In order to make each reference unique, these larger grids of 100 km by 100 km are given identifying letters. Thus, while the numerical part of the grid reference (476372) could be found on a number of OS

Grid reference 476372.

maps, adding the letters NT immediately places it in Southern Scotland and makes it unique. Another way of doing this is to add the map sheet number – there is only one 476372 on OS Landranger sheet 73.

You will have spotted that, while grid squares each have two-figure references for each side, the reference given has six figures. The extra figures are added to aid precise location finding, as can be seen from the illustration.

The identification of a particular grid square and any references within it always begins at its south-west (bottom left) corner. Thus, the house shown in the illustration is in grid square 4737. You always start with the easting, and then add the northing (an *aide-mémoire* often quoted is "along the passage and up the stairs"). So to identify the grid square, work your way *across* the map first, and then go *up*.

To give the more precise location using six figures, you have to imagine the square divided into tenths along each leg. These tenths are shown in the margin on 1:25 000 maps, but not on 1:50 000 maps. Estimating them is quite easy, and for most purposes, it wouldn't matter if you were slightly out.

Using this method, the house in the illustration is located at 476372. This identifies its location to within 100 metres in each direction. Surveyors and others needing very precise locations and working on large-scale maps often continue this process to give an eight-figure reference which is accurate to 10 m in each direction.

The national grid is a quick and convenient method of identifying any point on the map and conveying that information to others. You can use it when planning a route: if anyone else looks at that route, they can follow it without doubt

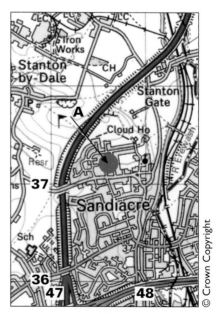

Illustration of grid reference 476372 on a map.

using the grid references. You can use it to arrange meetings – instead of giving complicated road directions, if you know the other person can read a map, you can just say "I'll meet you at the bridge at 516241, sheet 73". If you are going to meet someone who lives in the country, why not just ask them for the grid reference for their house, and use that as a guide? Try it with friends and relatives and see how you get on!

Larger features, such as a wood, for instance, cannot be identified by a six-figure reference. You therefore have to narrow your reference down to say, the north-east corner of the wood, or give merely the grid square – "we're heading for the wood in square 4732" will give a fair general direction.

Familiarity with grid references comes quickly with practice. Use them every time you plan a route or refer to a particular point and you will soon find that they become familiar and helpful aids to map-reading and finding your way around.

It is worth saying something here about triangulation pillars, those familiar squat concrete or stone truncated pyramids found all over the UK, most often on hilltops. The triangulation system has already been mentioned in Chapter 2. The pillars themselves are basically surveying tools at locations whose position can be exactly calculated. At least two other pillars should be visible from each one.

Most of the pillars we see today are of relatively recent construction – less than 100 years – and it is worth reflecting that the materials for most of them were carried up, often to a difficult, remote and high place, either on people's backs or sometimes by pony. There is a very solid foundation under the ground, and the pillar itself contains information which surveyors use, as well as the grooves on the top used for mounting a theodolite or other instrument.

There are regional variations – in the Highlands of Scotland, for instance, you find circular stone pillars. There are over 5000 "trig pillars" as they are popularly known in the UK, and in poor weather conditions they can be useful navigational aids. In terms of surveying, the vast majority are now redundant, their place having been taken by satellites circling the earth. Modern developments can leave them in odd places – at least one is now on the central reservation of a dual carriageway.

A few years ago the OS launched an exercise asking local people or clubs to "adopt" trig pillars so that they could be maintained in good condition. There was a huge response.

Triangulation – or "trig" pillar.

Considered objectively, we are talking about objects with little aesthetic appeal, but our trig pillars obviously have a firm place in our affections as walkers, and a substantial number are now cared for by local groups.

While this exercise was going on, an OS surveyor went to a very large field in East Anglia which was slightly higher than the surrounding countryside and was puzzled to find that the trig pillar clearly marked on the map at the centre of the field was missing. On enquiring with the farmer, he was told that "the damned thing was in the way of my ploughing, so I shifted it to the corner of the field". Fortunately this did not have too serious an effect, but in times past it could have dramatically affected the triangulation of the whole area!

8 USING A COMPASS

The first thing to be said about the compass is that, while it is a useful and important navigational aid and a great companion to the map, it is not a magic device that will get you out of trouble without fail. There are indeed times when having a compass and knowing how to use it can be vital for survival, but it is rare that the compass alone will do this: without some knowledge of your position on the map you cannot make full use of the compass.

By now, if you have been following the suggested exercises and practising your map-reading at every opportunity, you should be reasonably competent in reading the map, orientating yourself in the terrain, and recognising features around you and the way you are heading. The compass now comes into play to help you refine these skills and become more adept in route planning, measuring and estimating distance, and establishing your position.

The most useful type of compass is the protractor type as marketed by Silva, Suunto and other makers, and as shown in the illustration. It generally consists of the following parts:

A Silva protractor-type compass.

- A clear plastic baseplate, often marked with measuring scales on one or more sides and with a direction arrow.

- A small magnifier to help you pick out detail on the map.

- The compass dial, graduated in degrees from 0 to 360, with the four cardinal points of North, South, East and West clearly marked. The base of this dial has a number of parallel lines together with an arrow, often in red, aligned to North on the dial itself.

- The compass needle, floating in a liquid which acts as a 'damper' to help the needle settle more quickly and remain stable. The needle usually has a red and a white end; the red end always points to magnetic north.

When using a compass, you need to be aware that there are several different points all referred to as "North". True North is not usually shown on maps and for our purposes can be ignored. Grid North is the alignment of the north–south lines on maps which make up two sides of the grid squares. The compass, however, points to Magnetic North, which is a variable point on the earth's surface. It is currently in the Canadian Arctic, and is approximately 5.5° west of Grid North on maps of the UK. This variation is always given in the map legend; it is decreasing by about half a degree every five years. A small adjustment thus has to be made when taking a compass bearing, to allow for the difference between Grid North and Magnetic North. This is described more fully below.

One of the most frequent uses of a compass is to *take a bearing,* to help establish your direction of travel or to confirm your position in the landscape. The procedure for doing this is quite simple, as shown in the diagram.

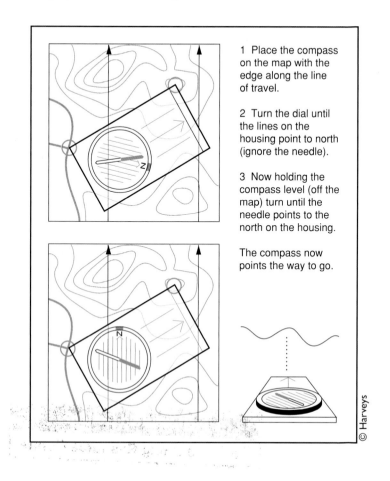

1 Place the compass on the map with the edge along the line of travel.

2 Turn the dial until the lines on the housing point to north (ignore the needle).

3 Now holding the compass level (off the map) turn until the needle points to the north on the housing.

The compass now points the way to go.

© Harveys

First, place the compass on the map so that the long edge is along the desired line of travel. If possible, link two points – your present position and either your destination or a point along the way to it – on the compass edge.

Next, keeping the compass edge between these two points, rotate the dial until the N for North lines up with the north lines on the map. The parallel lines on the base of the dial will confirm this alignment for you.

Next, make the adjustment for variation to Magnetic North. A good *aide-mémoire* for this is GUMA – Grid Unto Magnetic Add. So you add about 5° to your reading. (The reverse acronym is MUGS – Magnetic Unto Grid Subtract.)

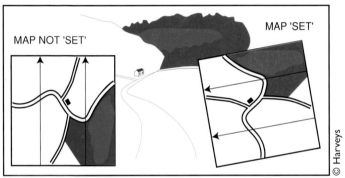

Setting the map to the terrain.

Now, hold the compass level in front of you and turn your whole body until the red end of the compass needle lines up with North on the dial. You are now facing your desired line of travel and can sight ahead to a good, fixed feature in the landscape along that line. Once you have this fixed feature you can walk to it, confident that you are following the right bearing. Once you reach the feature you are aiming for, you will need to take the bearing again and select another feature, and so on along your line of travel.

In clear visibility this is all good fun and no problem. In mist, heavy rain or driving snow it becomes another matter and you need to pay very close attention to the compass. Let us say that you are on a ridge which the map tells you heads west and leads you to the summit of the hill. Visibility is poor, and there are cliffs to either side.

In such conditions, you have to follow the bearing very carefully, constantly checking your line of travel, not with the map (unless there is a notable feature along the way), but with the compass. You may also have to measure the distance you need to travel and estimate how long that might take you, and even how many paces it will need. These are more advanced techniques beyond the scope of this book, but the basic skill of following a bearing carefully should be practised until it is second nature.

Very few people can follow a bearing with total accuracy. Most of us tend to drift off it to one side or another. An interesting little exercise, which is helpful in establishing which way you drift, is to find a large open space with no dangerous objects on it – a football or rugby pitch is ideal, provided it is not in use at the time!

Stand at one end and take a careful bearing on the goalpost at the other end. Set that bearing on the compass and set off *looking only at the compass* (you have to be strict about that). See how close to the goal post you end up. You can even if you want, and if you have somebody with you, put a large paper bag over your head and follow the compass inside it, so that you can't see out. It's a pound to a penny that even over this distance of about 100 m you'll be several metres out one way or the other.

Pace counting is affected by many factors:
A 100m distance mght be converted into the following pace count.

Footpath	120	A combination of these factors will lead
Gentle hill	140	to an even greater pace count.
Marshy ground	150	
Stony ground	150	Other factors will also have an effect -
Heather moorland	180	forest plantation, fatigue, backpack, wind,
Steep hill	200	and so on . . .

The compass can also be used to establish your position, in good visibility. Select two obvious features which you can readily identify from the map. Take bearings to them and once you have the bearing, lay the compass on the map and align it as described earlier, keeping the feature you selected on the long edge of the compass. Once the bearing matches up, draw a line along the long edge.

Do the same with the other feature, and where the lines intersect, that is your position. This method is not wholly accurate but can be useful in establishing to within reasonable limits where you are. Three points are better than two, and will often give you a small triangle within which you are standing.

The compass also helps you *set the map*, and orientate yourself in the landscape, a skill begun in Chapter 4. To do it using a compass is straightforward. Hold the compass ahead of you and swivel the dial so that the compass north arrow aligns with the arrow on the dial. Now place the compass on the map and turn the map until the north lines line up with the north lines on the compass. The map should now be "set" so that, for example, if you are on a road, the road on the map should stretch ahead of you as it does on the ground.

There are many other techniques with the compass – aiming off, using an "attack point" to get near to a feature, and so on. If you wish to learn more about them, there are good books on navigation which will help you.

A couple more points of which you should be aware: compasses are affected by metal objects, particularly those containing iron, and should never be left in the vicinity of such objects as the performance of the compass can deteriorate. Computers can also have an effect (placing a compass next to mine while typing this chapter caused the north arrow to swing through 180° and end up pointing south). Keep your compass safely in a place where nothing will affect its magnetic field.

In certain parts of the country, the rock can also affect compasses. This is notably true on the island of Skye, where compasses are not at all reliable in the mountains, but can also occur in other mountain areas.

The third point, perhaps less likely to concern you, is that in the southern hemisphere, everything is reversed. So if you take your compass for a walk in Australia or South Africa, and it is a northern hemisphere aligned model, you will need to use the south arrow to head north. It might be easier to buy a locally aligned compass to save awful confusion!

With these exceptions, the compass is an extremely reliable instrument – much more so than your brain. It is very common even for experienced mapreaders to set a bearing, look around and say to themselves "That *can't* be right". Invariably, it is, and by trusting the compass, you get to where you want to be. Your compass should be a trusted friend and ally, used with the map to help you get the maximum enjoyment from your outings.

9 ROUTE PLANNING

Being able to read a map is one thing: successfully planning a route is a skill of its own, but one that pays rich rewards in terms of both satisfaction as regards the route and enjoyment in gaining the most from your outings.

A good route is like a good book: it should have a proper beginning, middle and end. In some cases, of course, the start and finish will be the same, but the principle still applies. And just as a book is made up of chapters, so a route is made up of "legs", each of which requires some planning of itself. Generally speaking, the shorter the route, the fewer legs you will need.

A lot of fun can be had, and valuable experience gained, from simply planning routes at home using the map, without even going out. I spend hours doing this in the winter, plotting expeditions for the spring and summer ahead. Many of them never come to fruition, but that takes nothing away from the enjoyment derived from the planning, and it is all useful practice.

The principles of route planning apply whether you are walking, cycling, driving or using public transport, or a mixture of these options. Decide first of all where you are starting from and where you want to get to. Then start breaking the journey down into legs of appropriate length. If you are walking, make each leg no more than 5 km (3 miles): if cycling, perhaps 10 km (6 miles), and if driving, perhaps 32 km (20 miles). This chapter deals largely with walking/cycling journeys – route planning for car journeys is looked at in Chapter 10.

Look for significant points to act as the beginning and end of each leg. At the same time, look both for places or features you wish to visit or stop at along the way, and also at any obstacles on your route. Are there rivers to cross? If so, where are the bridges? If walking or cycling, are there hills in the way? If so, will you go over them (shorter but harder), or round them (longer but easier)? Any cliffs or other potentially dangerous obstacles?

You will soon find that the route begins to take shape. You will also almost certainly find that options present themselves for at least some of the legs, and these need to be graded according to preference. For example, a shorter but more exposed route

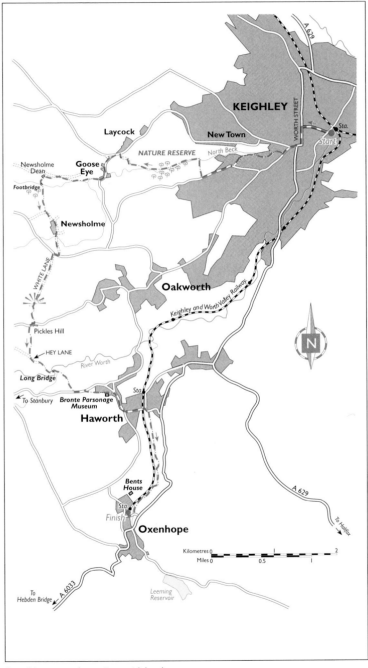

A walking route shown in a guidebook.

might be a good-weather option, with a longer but more sheltered alternative available. Or it might simply be the case that you will decide at point C whether you will divert before point D in order to see a waterfall.

This brings up the question of estimating time, which is another skill well worth acquiring. A rough guide can be given to start you off. If walking, 2–2.5 mph (about 4 kph) is reasonable going over good ground. Over rough or steep ground, that can reduce to 1.5 mph (2.5 kph) quite quickly. Cyclists can usually manage about 12 mph (20 kph) on good going, also reducing once off roads or over hills.

Once you have your route plotted in outline, measure it as carefully as you can and then try to estimate how long you think it will take you. Take into account the amount of climbing involved (you can do this by counting the contours) and any stops you wish to make, either for refreshments or to see

ROUTE CARD FEATURE	ROUTE	Direction	Distance	Climb	Time (min)
Car park					0
	Footpath	WNW	1100m	240m	
A Forest edge					30
	Footpath	SSW	950m	195m	
B Ridge					20
	Footpath to summit	NNW	1500m	300m	
C Summit					40
	Ridge No path, old fence	N	1250m	-210m	
D Saddle					20
	Footpath	E	1100m	-285m	
E Boulders					20
	Footpath (crossing two roads) Waterfall on left	ESE	1500m	-240m	
F Bridge					25
	Road	SSE	1400m	0	
G Car park					20
TOTALS:			8800m		175 mins

something in particular. Add 10 per cent for safety and you should have a reasonable time estimate. If it all adds up to more time than you have available, it is wiser to reduce the length of the expedition rather than try to cram it in and end up (a) exhausted and (b) dissatisfied because you had to miss things out.

At this stage you might like to make up a simple "route card" as shown in the illustration opposite. Put down each leg, where it starts and finishes, the distance, climbing if any, things to note along the way, obstacles, and any other information you think is relevant. This exercise can be very helpful in letting you see the route both as a whole and broken down into sections.

It is up to you whether you actually mark the route you wish to follow on your map(s) before going out. Not everyone feels it necessary to do this, but some people find it helpful. It also provides you with a record for the future.

However careful your planning, you will almost certainly find at some point that things go wrong while you are out. The first and most important rule is, to quote Corporal Jones in Dad's Army – "don't panic"! You may find that a footbridge which was a key point on your route is missing or unsafe; or a bus service you were relying on has been withdrawn.

Whatever the problem, take time to assess it and look for ways round it. If you are faced with an obstacle you can't get across or over, look for the best way round it to get back on your original route. You may have to decide which is the more important – the next leg, or simply reaching the finish? Don't be afraid to backtrack if that is the best way. Be certain of your position on the map at all times. What you must not do is crash on regardless, hoping against hope that a solution will magically present itself. It almost certainly won't, and you will end up in more difficulty.

Remember the guiding principle that the map is your friend and is there to help you. Getting out of a "little local difficulty" should be as much fun as planning the route was in the first place. If you are leading a group, be it your family or a walking club, don't be afraid to ask advice. Many groups have got into unnecessary trouble simply because the leader's pride wouldn't let him admit he had gone wrong or was uncertain of his position. Discuss the situation sensibly and a solution will arise.

The intention in raising these matters is not to be alarmist, but it is as well to accept that at some point you may find that your plans don't quite work out. You will learn from the experience.

It is sensible in any case to retain some flexibility. For instance, if you are unexpectedly ahead of schedule and everyone is feeling fit, you can add a diversion to another viewpoint or hilltop which might not have been in your original plans. Conversely, if the weather is bad and people are not enjoying themselves, don't press on regardless simply because you have planned a particular route. There's always another day.

The emphasis should be on fun and enjoyment throughout. Get everyone involved from the start in the route planning, making suggestions, working out legs, identifying significant points, and so on. Share the responsibility of "leading". Youngsters in particular will enjoy this, and it's easy enough to keep an eye on them in case they go wrong. If they do, explain calmly what has happened and show them, using the map (this applies to adults too, of course!).

You will be surprised how quickly your route-planning skills develop, and probably surprised at how often you use them. Life is a series of routes and the better our planning, the more we are likely to get out of it all.

10 USING ROAD MAPS

A simple question to start this chapter. Have you ever read your Road Atlas? Be honest, now! Most of us have Road Atlases at home or in the car, but how often do we actually use them properly? Very rarely , I would suggest. Yet they contain masses of helpful information put there in order to help us plan our journeys.

Using the Road Atlas, you can either make your journey swift and efficient, or slower and more interesting – or a mixture of the two. You can work out your distance and thus calculate the likely fuel use, and also how long the journey will take you.

A personal example worth quoting was a drive from home in the Scottish Borders to Manchester. The aim was not a scenic trip, but a fast journey. The route itself was no problem, and was quite straightforward (A7 to Carlisle, M6/M61 to Manchester) but my guess as to how far it was turned out to be some way out, and that combined with roadworks led to an unnecessarily high

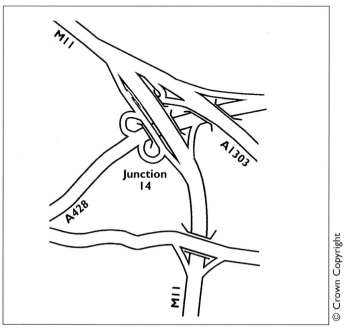

© Crown Copyright

Stylised motorway map.

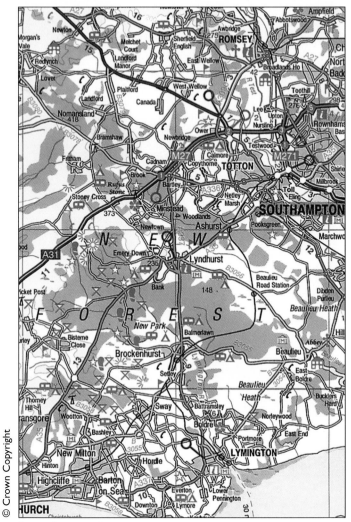

Extract from a road map.

level of anxiety towards the end of the journey. A few minutes with a Road Atlas the evening before would readily have established how far the journey was, thus enabling sufficient time to be allowed, with a margin of error for the unexpected built in.

It's as if we don't somehow regard a Road Atlas as containing "real" maps. But they do, and are, moreover, maps drawn for a specific purpose. You don't expect road maps to show all the terrain detail that the Landranger or Pathfinder maps show. What you want is for the road network to be clearly shown, with the roads classified, and distances between key points given, to enable you to plan your journey.

In fact you often get much more than that. The AA's Road Atlas of Britain, for instance, provides detailed town plans, lists of local radio stations which give traffic news, a map of the motorway network with likely "bottlenecks", and another map, stylised along the lines of the London Underground map on p. 2, showing all the service stations on motorways and main trunk roads – a great help especially to families undertaking long road journeys.

Road journeys, unless they are either very local or very familiar, should be planned as carefully as your expeditions on foot or cycle. Very much the same principles apply – note down start and finish points and break the journey into "legs", ending each leg either at a service station/refreshment stop or for a change of driver.

If you have time available, have a look at the Road Atlas and think about taking a different route, to visit somewhere interesting along the way or simply to break up the tedium of motorway driving. Most road maps show main tourist attractions; if possible, take larger-scale maps as well. The OS offer intermediate scale Routemaster maps which are very helpful in planning longer journeys.

The symbols used in most Road Atlases are already familiar: blue for motorways, red for major A-roads, yellow or brown for minor roads, and so on. The extra information is in the form of road numbers, mileage between key points, service stations and the like. These atlases are designed to be easy to read, and many now come with a large page format which means that a single spread covers quite a big area.

One of the keys to an interesting and friction-free journey is to involve everybody in planning it and carrying it out. Passengers can also act as navigators, and if you have more than one passenger, rotate the navigational duties so that everyone gets a shot. The navigator can tell others about things to watch out for or point them out as they are passed, but his or her main duty is to keep the driver on the right road, alerting the driver to all junctions, roundabouts etc. in good time.

If you have a journey that you make frequently, say to a friend or relative, there's almost certainly another way of getting there that you haven't tried yet. This is simply because, when we get in our cars, a sort of "automatic pilot" takes over and we follow the familiar route without thinking too much about it. Next time, have another look at the atlas. B-roads are always worth a try, and providing you leave in plenty of time, even if the route turns out to be less good than your usual one, you will at least have tried it out. You may find it's a real gem.

On long journeys there are likely to be three or four viable alternatives, depending on the time available. Our motorway network is not yet so comprehensive that we can get everywhere using the "blue roads". One example from personal experience was taking two completely different routes in and out of Pembrokeshire in west Wales from the Manchester area, and enjoying them both. It made the trip more satisfying than simply retracing the inward route on the way out.

Using road maps is just as good practice and experience as using any other type of map, provided you do the job properly. Don't leave your Road Atlas sitting forlornly on the back shelf of the car, its covers curling up in the sun. Make it earn its keep, and you'll be surprised at the opportunities it opens up, and probably the time it saves you as well.

Another advantage of Road Atlases is that they are reprinted every year, which isn't possible with larger-scale maps. Roads do change remarkably quickly, and many of us will have been caught out by using an out-of-date atlas which didn't show a new bypass or – and this is also common – a change of road number. It's worth the small investment to get a new atlas each year. A hint around Christmas time should bring one!

This chapter should have shown that it is worth making more use, more often, of your Road Atlas. Have a look at it now and see what interesting information it offers you. There will be things in there you have never looked at and which can help you get the most out of future journeys. Anything which increases the enjoyment and satisfaction of driving is well worth while, and the Road Atlas can certainly do that – if you give it the chance.

11 RIGHTS OF WAY AND ACCESS

There is one group of symbols on large-scale maps that we have not yet looked at – those depicting public rights of way. It is important that these are understood, as they are a great help in planning your routes whether you are walking, cycling or indeed on horseback.

The map legend shows four types of right of way in England and Wales. These are:

- public footpaths (red dots)
- public bridleways (red dashes)
- roads used as a public path (red dot/dash pattern)
- byways open to all traffic (red dot/cross pattern)

Public footpaths are just that: routes, often across open country, which can be followed on foot. They are not open for horses, cycles, or any other wheeled traffic.

Public bridleways are routes which are open to walkers, cyclists and equestrians.

Roads used as a public path (RUPPs) are minor highways which have retained their historical status as vehicular rights of way, though only rarely used as such, but are also open as footpaths.

Byways open to all traffic (BOATs) are often "green lanes" through the countryside which have similar rights to bridleways but can also be used by vehicles.

The last two categories, RUPPs and BOATs, are being reviewed as this book is published, and their status, or the means of showing them on OS maps, may change. The OS are also introducing symbols to show what they call "white roads", which are little-used roads and tracks also open as walking, cycling or riding routes, though not legally defined as public rights of way.

It is important that the distinction between footpaths and bridleways is understood and observed. The principle is that the greater use (i.e. horse-riding or cycling) always includes the lesser (walking) but not the reverse. This can cause some anguish to cyclists and equestrians, but bridleways are generally more robust and able to cope with the mixed traffic they carry. The South Downs Way path, for instance, is a bridleway for the whole of its length, whereas the Pennine Way is for the most part only a footpath, crossing as it does much higher, softer and more sensitive ground for long sections.

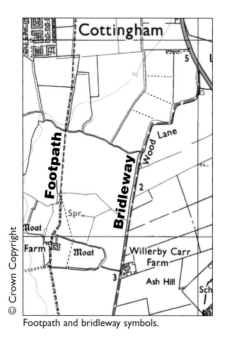

Footpath and bridleway symbols.

Careful study of OS maps will enable you to work out routes using footpaths and bridleways, as appropriate. The map also shows other paths and tracks, but unless they carry the red symbol, they are not recognised as rights of way and the public therefore has no right of access to them.

We have a dense network of public rights of way totalling many thousands of kilometres. Those shown on the present maps were for the most part defined after the passing of the National Parks and Access to the Countryside Act in 1949. Under this Act, all local authorities were required to produce what are called "definitive maps" of public rights of way. These maps, which should be regularly updated, are held at council offices and are open to inspection by any interested party. The definitive maps are used as the basis for showing public rights of way on all up-to-date large-scale maps.

The network is dynamic in that paths are created, diverted or closed all the time, for example through building developments, alterations to field patterns, or because new routes have been negotiated. All creations, diversions and closures have to be advertised locally and if there are objections a public inquiry may be held. Organisations such as the Ramblers Association are vigilant in protecting rights of way, and the work they do is vitally important, as without it, many routes could be lost.

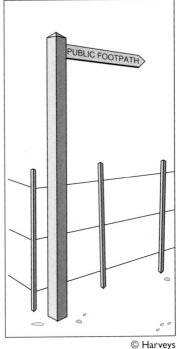

© Harveys

Local authorities have a duty to signpost rights of way at all points where they leave the public highway. Some years ago, the Countryside Commission, aware that many footpaths and bridleways were obstructed or otherwise unusable, launched a campaign to have them all open by the year 2000. Inevitably, this will be achieved in some areas but not in others.

If you try to follow a right of way on the map and find it blocked or otherwise unusable on the ground, you should in the first instance (assuming you are certain of your position on the right of way) report the matter to the Rights of Way Officer in your local council. You might also like to inform the local Ramblers Association group, whose address you should be able to locate through the public library. If you are on a right of way and find it blocked, you have the right to remove the obstacle sufficiently to enable you to progress, but you might feel safer simply reporting the obstruction – few of us carry wire cutters or saws around with us!

Rights of way are important everywhere, but perhaps especially over agricultural land. Here too it is particularly important that you follow them, so as not to disturb farming activities unduly. In the uplands and on open hill and moorland, there is a generally good freedom of access, but here too you will find many rights of way marked. Some of these are major routes known as National Trails, and these are named as such on OS maps. Examples include the Pennine Way, the North and South Downs Ways, the Ridgeway and Offa's Dyke Path. You

can get a map of National Trails from the Countryside Commission (address in Chapter 13).

The situation in Scotland is rather different. Here, rights of way, although they certainly exist in considerable numbers, are not marked as such on OS maps, which can make things a little difficult for the visitor looking for guidance. There is, however, a general acceptance of public access to the countryside in

Scotland, provided that responsible behaviour is observed, especially at sensitive times such as the peak grouse and stag shooting seasons (mid August to late October) and at lambing time in the spring.

Tourist Information Centres, and sometimes local councils, should be able to give you information on local walks in Scotland. There are also many excellent guidebooks, such as the The Stationery Office (formerly HMSO) "25 Walks" series, which can safely be used. OS maps of Scotland show many paths and tracks, but these cannot always be followed on the ground, so if you are unfamiliar with the area, it is perhaps better to take the advice of others who have worked out routes for you to follow.

There are at present three National Trails in Scotland, the West Highland Way, Speyside Way and Southern Upland Way, and a small number of others are being developed. Many areas, such as Dunkeld and Pitlochry in Perthshire, have well-developed local path networks with very good accompanying literature, providing plenty of opportunities for visitors. Forest Enterprise also have a host of walking routes in their extensive forests.

Off-road cyclists and equestrians in Scotland are less well off legally, but with a rich network of tracks on the ground, have plenty of places to explore without undue difficulty.

In Northern Ireland, access is generally by negotiation with estates, landowners and farmers, and a path network is gradually evolving. Some areas, such as the Mourne Mountains, are well provided for, and there are also many paths around Belfast. Here again, look for local guidance in the form of books and leaflets, or ask at Tourist Information Centres.

This is a necessarily brief overview of the access situation. If you wish to find out more, you could try contacting the Rights of Way Officer in your local council, and also, especially in England and Wales, the relevant organisations such as the Ramblers Association, the Cyclists Touring Club and the British Horse Society. Their addresses are given in Chapter 13.

countries there can be difficulties with interpreting symbols and legends written in a totally unfamiliar alphabet and style.

If you are travelling abroad and would like to try to get maps of the area you are visiting, there are several ways of going about it. You can try one of the distributors in the UK who specialise in foreign maps (see Chapter 13 for addresses). They are experts in their field and will give you good advice.

You can also try to find maps produced here in the UK. Several UK-based companies have large ranges of maps of foreign countries, including though not exclusively those most often visited by tourists. You should find these maps in the travel section of large bookshops. There are helpful series which concentrate on major cities – not just places such as Paris and Berlin but also more exotic locations including Cairo and Hong Kong.

You will often find that the maps you can obtain are at a much smaller scale than those you have become familiar with in the UK. It is understandably not economic for UK companies to either produce or stock full ranges of large-scale maps of other countries, even if they can obtain them. Don't be put off by this. It is still more helpful to have a small-scale map than to have no map at all.

Another and somewhat more adventurous way of getting foreign maps is by dealing with the mapping agency or a distributor in the country itself. In this case you will probably have to be able to correspond in the language of the country, but if you can, you may well be rewarded by getting just the maps you need.

There are also good guidebook series (Sunflower is one) which provide very helpful information, show both car tours and walks, and include maps. These guides cover many popular holiday destinations around the Mediterranean, and further afield. Using them feels the same as using a guide to an area of the UK you are unfamiliar with: someone else has done the legwork and provided you with the information you need.

The aim in including this short chapter is to encourage you to try to get some sort of map for every country or area that you visit. You will enjoy using them and looking at them after you return to remind you of places you have seen. After experience of some foreign maps, you may realise how fortunate we are in the UK to have such truly excellent national map coverage. It is something we should never take for granted.

USEFUL ADDRESSES

British Horse Society, British Equestrian Centre, Stoneleigh, Kenilworth CV8 2LR.

Countryside Commission, John Dower House, Crescent Place, Cheltenham GL50 3RA.

Cyclists Touring Club, Cotterell House, 69 Meadrow, Godalming GU7 3HS.

Forestry Commission, 231 Corstorphine Road, Edinburgh EH12 7AT.

National Trust, 36 Queen Anne's Gate, London SW1H OAS.

National Trust for Scotland, 5 Charlotte Square, Edinburgh EH2 4DU.

Ramblers Association, 1-5 Wandsworth Road, London SW8 2XX.

Scottish Natural Heritage, 12 Hope Terrace, Edinburgh EH9 2AS.

Scottish Rights of Way Society, John Cotton Business Centre, 11 Sunnyside, Easter Road, Edinburgh EH7 5RA.

MAP PRODUCERS AND DISTRIBUTORS

Cordee, 3a de Montfort Street, Leicester LE1 7HD.

Harvey Map Services Ltd, 12-16 Main Street, Doune, Perthshire FK6 6BJ.

Ordnance Survey, Romsey Road, Maybush, Southampton SO9 4DH. Customer information helpline: 01703 792912.

The National Map Centre, 22-24 Caxton Street, London SW1H OQU.

The Map Shop, 15 High Street, Upton on Severn WR8 OHJ.

Stanfords, 12-14 Long Acre, London WC2E 9LP.

Maps by Mail, PO Box 350A, Surbiton KT5 9LX.

INDEX

The Stationery
Office

Published by The Stationery Office and available from:

The Stationery Office Bookshops
71 Lothian Road, Edinburgh EH3 9AZ
(counter service only)
59-60 Holborn Viaduct, London EC1A 2FD
(temporary location: counter service and fax orders only)
Fax 0171-831 1326
68-69 Bull Street, Birmingham B4 6AD
0121-236 9696 Fax 0121-236 9699
33 Wine Street, Bristol BS1 2BQ
0117-926 4306 Fax 0117-929 4515
9-21 Princess Street, Manchester M60 8AS
0161-834 7201 Fax 0161-833 0634
16 Arthur Street, Belfast BT1 4GD
01232 238451 Fax 01232 235401
The Stationery Office Oriel Bookshop
The Friary, Cardiff CF1 4AA
01222 395548 Fax 01222 384347

The Stationery Office publications are also available from:

The Publications Centre
(mail, telephone and fax orders only)
PO Box 276, London SW8 5DT
General enquiries 0171-873 0011
Telephone orders 0171-873 9090
Fax orders 0171-873 8200

Accredited Agents
(see Yellow Pages)

and through good booksellers

Printed in Scotland for The Stationery Office Limited J12514, C50, 12/97, CCN 070343'